Lerner SPORTS™

ULTIMATE SPORTS STATS

PRO SOCCER BY THE NUMBERS

Percy Leed

Lerner Publications ◆ Minneapolis

Statistics are accurate through October 2023 unless otherwise noted.

Lerner Publications Company
An imprint of Lerner Publishing Group, Inc.
241 First Avenue North
Minneapolis, MN 55401 USA

For reading levels and more information, look up this title at www.lernerbooks.com.

Main body text set in Adrianna.
Typeface provided by Chank.

Designer: Viet Chu
Lerner team: Sue Marquis

Library of Congress Cataloging-in-Publication Data

Names: Leed, Percy, 1968– author.
Title: Pro soccer by the numbers / Percy Leed.
Description: Minneapolis : Lerner Publications, 2025. | Series: Lerner sports. Ultimate sports stats | Includes bibliographical references and index. | Audience: Ages 7–11 | Audience: Grades 4–6 | Summary: "Soccer is one of the world's most popular sports. Fans can keep up with soccer's intense competition through stats. From assists to goals to epic saves, explore the stats of soccer's best teams and players"— Provided by publisher.
Identifiers: LCCN 2023048826 (print) | LCCN 2023048827 (ebook) | ISBN 9798765625972 (library binding) | ISBN 9798765629895 (paperback) | ISBN 9798765638248 (epub)
Subjects: LCSH: Soccer—Juvenile literature. | Soccer—Statistics—Juvenile literature.
Classification: LCC GV943.25 .L449 2025 (print) | LCC GV943.25 (ebook) | DDC 796.334—dc23/eng/20231021

LC record available at https://lccn.loc.gov/2023048826
LC ebook record available at https://lccn.loc.gov/2023048827

Manufactured in the United States of America
1-1010070-51931-2/13/2024

TABLE OF CONTENTS

INTRODUCTION

SPANNING THE GLOBE

Soccer is one of the world's most popular sports. Top players in the US and Canada compete in Major League Soccer (MLS). Since 2012, the National Women's Soccer League (NWSL) has opened the field to women pro players in the US.

Soccer is called football nearly everywhere else in the world. There are more than 3.5 billion soccer fans worldwide. People have played in the Football Association Challenge Cup in England since 1871. It is the oldest soccer competition in the world.

2022 NWSL CHAMPIONSHIPS

WORLD TOURNAMENTS

The Fédération Internationale de Football Association (FIFA) is in charge of soccer around the world. Every four years, a different country holds the FIFA World Cup. Many people consider the World Cup to be the top prize in soccer.

Soccer has been part of the Olympic Games since 1900. Since the 1990s, women have had their own FIFA World Cup and Olympic tournaments.

STATS IN SOCCER

With more people getting involved in soccer, it can be tough to keep up. But one way fans can stay in touch with their favorite teams and players is through stats. Check out some of soccer's greatest stats!

1930 FIFA WORLD CUP

CHAPTER 1

PLAYER STATS

HINATA MIYAZAWA

THE GOLDEN BOOT

Scoring goals takes a lot of skill and luck. The person who scores the most goals in a tournament wins the Golden Boot award. In 2023, Japan's Hinata Miyazawa took home the Golden Boot at the FIFA Women's World Cup.

RECENT WOMEN'S WORLD CUP GOLDEN BOOT WINNERS

YEAR	PLAYER	TEAM	GOALS
2023	Hinata Miyazawa	Japan	5
2019	Megan Rapinoe	United States	6
2015	Célia Šašić	Germany	6
2011	Homare Sawa	Japan	5
2007	Marta	Brazil	7

PREMIER EVENT

England's top soccer league is the Premier League. It started in 1992. Alan Shearer is the Premier League's all-time leading goal scorer. He played for Newcastle United at St. James' Park. In 2016, the league honored him with a statue that stands at the park.

ALAN SHEARER

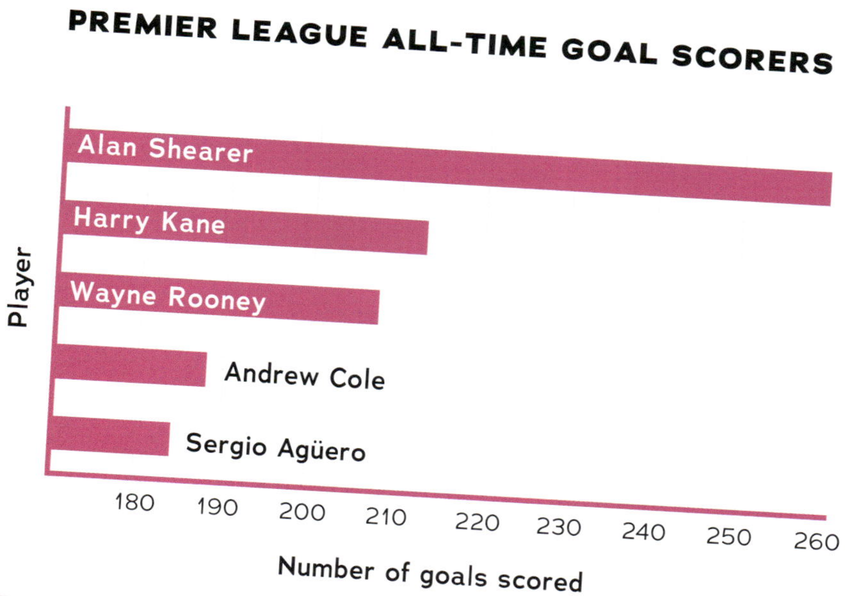

LIONEL MESSI

WINNING THE PICHICHI TROPHY

Spain's top pro soccer league, La Liga, has many star players. The player who leads the league in goals scored for the season wins the Pichichi Trophy. Cristiano Ronaldo has won it three times. Telmo Zarra won it six times. Lionel Messi has won it eight times, the most for any player in history.

MOST GOALS SCORED IN A LA LIGA SEASON		
PLAYER	TEAM	GOALS
Lionel Messi	Barcelona	50
Cristiano Ronaldo	Real Madrid	48
Lionel Messi	Barcelona	46
Cristiano Ronaldo	Real Madrid	46
Lionel Messi	Barcelona	43

WAIT, WHAT!?

La Liga has held 92 championships since its first season in 1929. Real Madrid and Barcelona have together won over 60 of them.

THE ULTIMATE GOAL

Scoring a goal in any game is exciting. But scoring on the world's biggest soccer stage turns you into a superstar. Miroslav Klose did it five times during the 2002 World Cup. He scored five times at the World Cup in 2006, four times in 2010, and twice in 2014.

MIROSLAV KLOSE

TOP GOAL SCORERS IN WORLD CUP HISTORY

CARLI LLOYD

MORE THAN A HAT TRICK

One player scoring three goals in a game is called a hat trick. It is a rare feat. But members of the United States Women's National Team (USWNT) have done even better. Nine USWNT players have scored five goals in a game.

MOST GOALS IN A GAME BY A USWNT PLAYER SINCE 2012			
PLAYER	**GOALS**	**SEASON**	**OPPONENT**
Carli Lloyd	5	2021	Paraguay
Alex Morgan	5	2019	Thailand
Crystal Dunn	5	2016	Puerto Rico
Sydney Leroux	5	2012	Guatemala
Amy Rodriguez	5	2012	Dominican Republic

WAIT, WHAT!?

In 1930, US player Bert Patenaude scored the first hat trick in a World Cup.

MAKING THE PLAY

Assists happen when a teammate helps another player on their team score a goal. Coaches often put their best passers at the midfielder position. This allows midfielders to pass the ball toward forwards, who are often the main scorers.

CARLOS VALDERRAMA

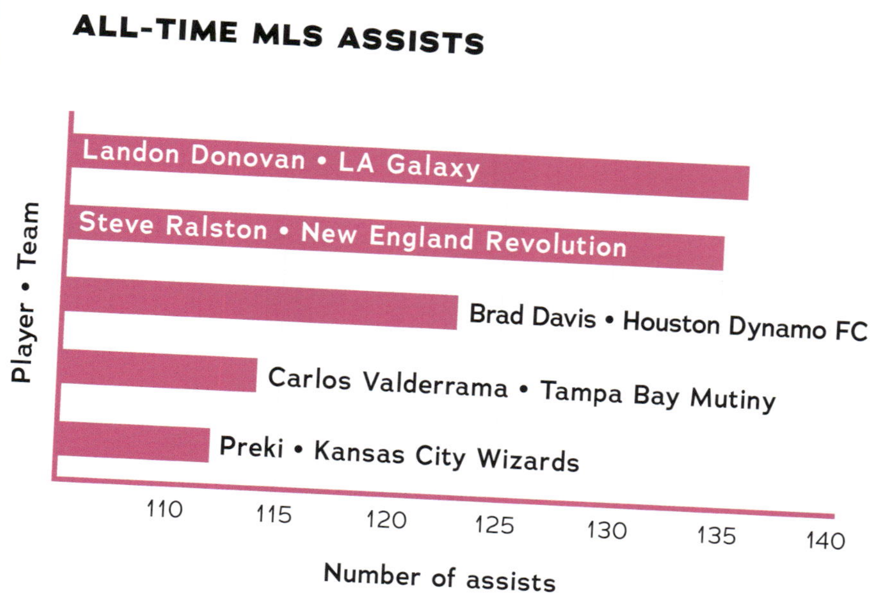

Passing Fancy

A player can make a great pass, but sometimes their teammates aren't so good at scoring. How does this affect their stats?

Soccer leagues use lots of stats to judge the skills of passers. Stats such as assists (A) are considered. So is the percentage of passes completed successfully (P%).

THIAGO ALMADA

TOP MLS PASSERS IN 2023

PLAYER	TEAM	A	P%
Thiago Almada	Atlanta United	19	84.1
Héctor Herrera	Houston Dynamo FC	17	86.4
Carles Gil	New England Revolution	15	83.8
Luciano Acosta	FC Cincinnati	14	74.8
Eduard Löwen	St. Louis City SC	14	74.3

THAT'S THE POINT

Some players can score from anywhere on the field. Others are great at knowing where their teammates are going to be and then pass them the ball. The best players can do both.

Fans use points to keep track of a league's top players. A goal is worth two points. An assist is worth one point.

LANDON DONOVAN

US MEN'S NATIONAL TEAM ALL-TIME POINTS LEADERS

PLAYER	GOALS	ASSISTS	POINTS
Landon Donovan	57	58	172
Clint Dempsey	57	21	135
Jozy Altidore	42	14	98
Eric Wynalda	34	16	84
Brian McBride	30	10	70

STEFAN FREI

SHUTOUTS

The goalkeepers in MLS are among the world's top athletes. The best goalkeepers stop the opposing team from scoring in a game. When the other team doesn't score, the goalkeeper earns a shutout.

2023 REGULAR SEASON MLS SHUTOUT LEADERS

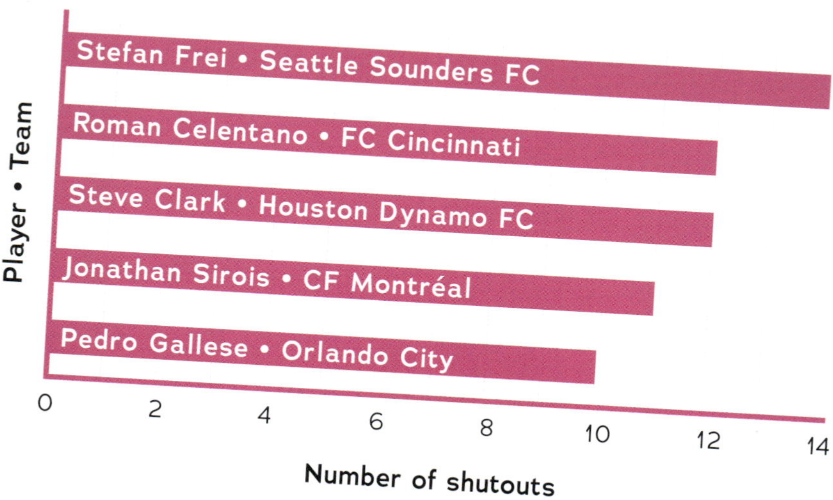

THE GOLDEN GLOVE

Goalkeepers have a tough job. The best players go on to win the Golden Glove. This award is given to goalkeepers with the best overall performance at a tournament. At the 2023 World Cup, Mary Earps of England won the Golden Glove with three shutouts.

RECENT WOMEN'S WORLD CUP GOLDEN GLOVE WINNERS

YEAR	PLAYER	TEAM	SHUTOUTS
2023	Mary Earps	England	3
2019	Sari van Veenendaal	Netherlands	3
2015	Hope Solo	United States	5
2011	Hope Solo	United States	2
2007	Nadine Angerer	Germany	6

MIA HAMM

TIP OF THE CAP

In soccer's early years, teammates weren't required to wear the same jersey. Instead, they wore matching caps. Players no longer wear caps during games. But the term *cap* still represents playing in an international match.

PLAYERS WITH THE MOST USWNT CAPS

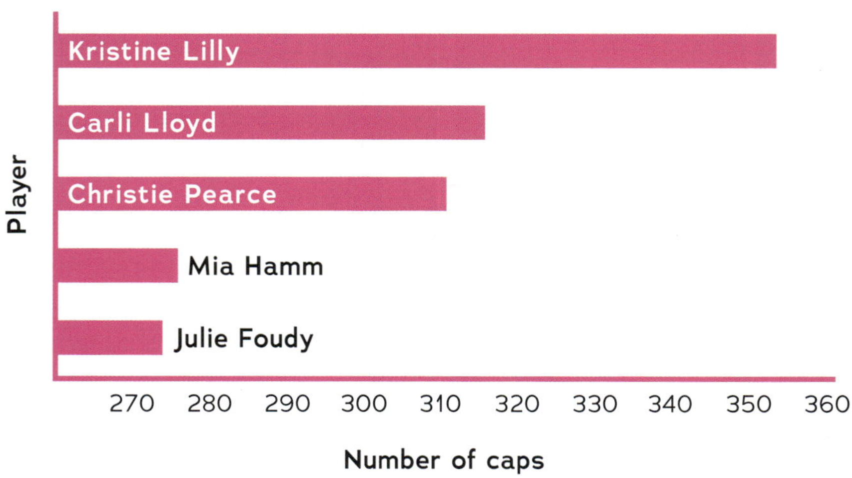

CHAPTER 2

TEAM STATS

ARGENTINA PLAYERS AT THE 2022 MEN'S WORLD CUP

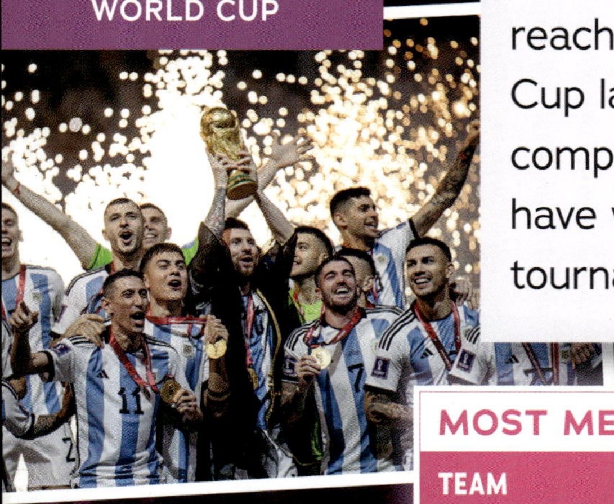

RAISING THE CUP

As many as 200 national teams compete in qualifying matches to reach the Men's World Cup. The World Cup lasts one month, and 32 teams compete for the trophy. Nine nations have won the World Cup since the first tournament in 1930.

MOST MEN'S WORLD CUP WINS

TEAM	WINS	YEARS WON
Brazil	5	1958, 1962, 1970, 1994, 2002
Italy	4	1934, 1938, 1982, 2006
West Germany	4	1954, 1974, 1990
Argentina	3	1978, 1986, 2022
Uruguay	2	1930, 1950

WAIT, WHAT!?

Brazil is the only country to have qualified for all 22 World Cup tournaments.

NEYMAR

STRIKING GOLD!

Neymar scored the winning penalty kick for Brazil at the 2016 Olympic Games. It was Brazil's first Olympic gold medal in soccer. Brazil became the 19th country to win the men's gold since soccer became an Olympic sport in 1900. Then they won gold again in 2021 at the Olympics in Tokyo, Japan.

COUNTRIES WITH THE MOST OLYMPIC GOLD MEDALS FOR MEN'S SOCCER

Great Britain
1900, 1908, 1912

Hungary
1952, 1964, 1968

Brazil
2016, 2020

Argentina
2004, 2008

Soviet Union
1956, 1988

US WOMEN LEAD THE WORLD

The USWNT formed in 1985. It is the most successful women's soccer team in the world. The USWNT has won more big matches and scored more goals than any other team in women's soccer history. It has also had longer winning streaks and collected more gold medals than any other team worldwide.

WOMEN'S WORLD CUP CHAMPIONS

COUNTRY	WORLD CUP TITLES	YEARS
United States	4	1991, 1999, 2015, 2019
Germany	2	2003, 2007
Spain	1	2023
Japan	1	2011
Norway	1	1995

WOMEN'S OLYMPIC CHAMPIONS

COUNTRY	OLYMPIC GOLD MEDALS	YEARS
United States	4	1996, 2004, 2008, 2012
Canada	1	2020
Germany	1	2016
Norway	1	2000

WAIT, WHAT!?

The USWNT won the first Women's World Cup in 1991 by beating Norway 2–1. The US team had beaten its previous five opponents by a combined score of 49–0.

YOU CAN'T SCORE IF YOU DON'T SHOOT

The number of shots per game (SPG) a team takes is an important stat. It helps coaches and fans understand how well a team plays. But many of those shots may miss their target.

An even more important number is shots on goal per game (SGPG). This stat tells fans how many shots would have been goals if the other team hadn't stopped them.

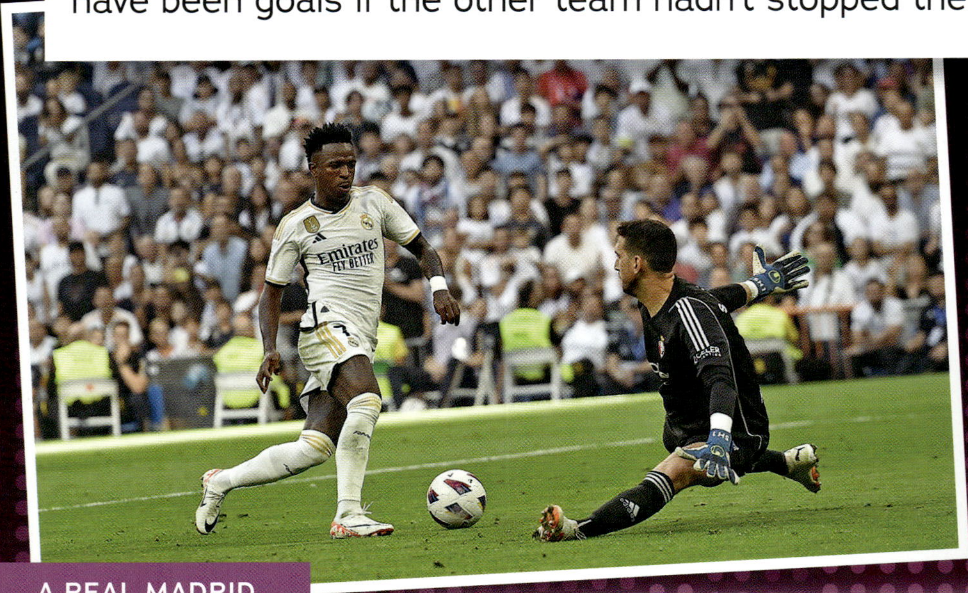

A REAL MADRID PLAYER (*LEFT*) TAKES A SHOT.

TOP SHOOTING TEAMS IN LA LIGA IN 2022–2023

TEAM	SPG	SGPG
Real Madrid	16.7	5.4
Barcelona	15	4.9
Atlético Madrid	14.2	5.1
Athletic Club	14.2	4.1
Rayo Vallecano	13.4	3.8

CREATING WAYS TO SCORE

Soccer teams score in different ways. Most goals (G) are scored when players kick them into the net. Others are headed goals (HG). A headed goal is when a player hits the ball into the net with their head. A team might also have a great shooter who can score a penalty kick goal (PKG). A penalty kick occurs after some fouls. A player can kick the ball at the net with only the goalkeeper to guard it.

COLUMBUS CREW FORWARD CUCHO HERNÁNDEZ (*CENTER*)

HOW THE TOP MLS TEAMS SCORED IN 2023

TEAM	G	HG	PKG
Columbus Crew	67	6	7
Atlanta United	66	13	2
St. Louis City SC	62	12	5
New England Revolution	58	7	3
FC Cincinnati	57	6	8

NASHVILLE SC DEFENDER LUKAS MACNAUGHTON (*RIGHT*) FIGHTS FOR THE BALL IN 2023.

DE-FENSE! DE-FENSE!

When it comes to defense, the most important stat is the number of goals an opponent scores against your team. It tells the story of how a team's entire defense comes together to stop opponents from scoring. The lower the number, the better.

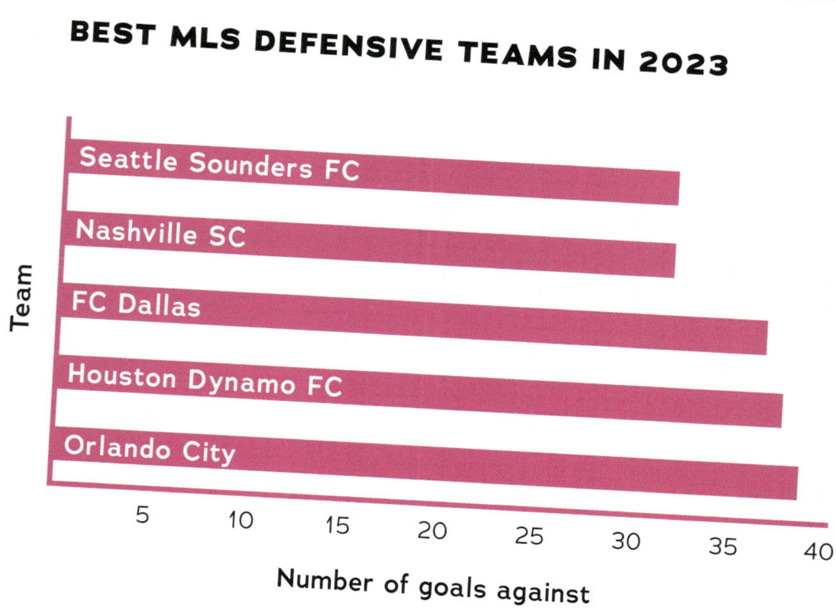

Fierce Defense

Teams work hard to prevent the other team from scoring. Though sometimes they try a little too hard. A strong tackle can stop a goal-scoring chance before it starts. But rough plays can lead to fouls if players aren't careful. The best defenders walk a thin line between fierce tackling and getting too many fouls.

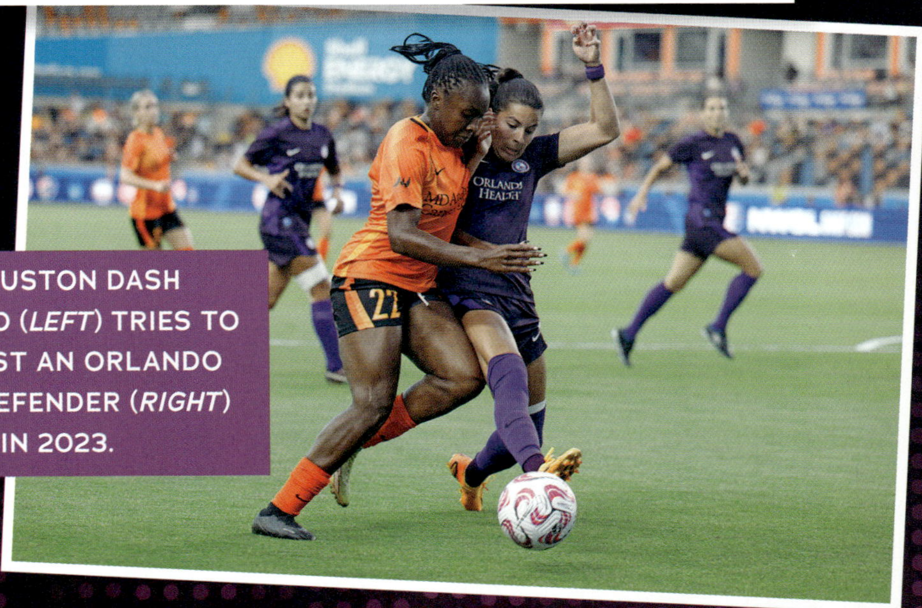

A HOUSTON DASH FORWARD (*LEFT*) TRIES TO GET PAST AN ORLANDO PRIDE DEFENDER (*RIGHT*) IN 2023.

NWSL'S TOP TACKLING TEAMS IN 2023

TEAM	TACKLES PER GAME	FOULS PER GAME
Orlando Pride	20.6	10.6
Portland Thorns FC	20	7.3
Angel City FC	18.8	10.6
Gotham FC	18.3	10.9
OL Reign	18.1	10.4

CHAPTER 3

STATS ARE HERE TO STAY

MATCH STATS

The rules of soccer have changed over time, but fans have always looked to stats to tell the stories of the sport. An 1866 match in England between teams from Sheffield and London was the first official game to last 90 minutes. (Modern matches still last 90 minutes.) Stats from the match were recorded in a box score. The numbers told who scored goals and when they were scored.

THE BOX SCORE

The modern box score contains much more info than it did in 1866. Take a look at the box score on the next page to see an account of the 2023 Women's World Cup semifinal match between Spain and Sweden. It has all the stats a fan wants to know about a soccer match. What do all these words and numbers mean? Use the key on the next page to read the box score.

2023 WORLD CUP SEMIFINAL MATCH
SPAIN 2, SWEDEN 1

COUNTRY	SCORER	WHEN SCORED
Spain	Salma Paralluelo	81st minute
Sweden	Rebecka Blomqvist	88th minute
Spain	Olga Carmona	89th minute

KEY
SA = shots attempted
SOG = shots on goal
FC = fouls committed
CK = corner kicks
SV = saves

SPAIN	
SA	13
SOG	2
FC	6
CK	3
SV	2

SWEDEN	
SA	6
SOG	3
FC	13
CK	3
SV	0

SWEDEN'S STINA BLACKSTENIUS (*LEFT*) AND SPAIN'S JENNIFER HERMOSO (*CENTER*)

MEMBERS OF REAL MADRID GATHER TO LISTEN TO THEIR HEAD COACH.

STAT STRATEGY

Fans love to follow the stats of their favorite teams and players around the world. But soccer teams use stats too. Players use stats to plan for opponents. For example, defenders know if a player is likely to pass or shoot based on their stats. Then they use that information to try to stop them.

Coaches use stats to come up with game plans. Perhaps a team's next opponent often scores on the counterattack. Then the coach may order their defenders to stay closer than usual to their own goal.

FANTASY AND THE FUTURE

Fantasy soccer is wildly popular in Europe. It's also growing in the US and Canada. Fantasy soccer is a contest that adult fans play using the stats of real players. To play, fans choose players from leagues such as MLS to form fantasy teams. Most fantasy games are played online.

Websites and TV networks around the world look at soccer stats and give advice for fantasy players. One study showed that 62.5 million people in the US and Canada played fantasy sports in 2022. The number of people playing fantasy soccer is growing!

STATS MATCHUP

Most soccer fans around the world agree that Lionel Messi and Cristiano Ronaldo are the two best soccer players in the sport. Messi played for a long time in La Liga for FC Barcelona. He's also the star player on Argentina's national team. When he races around the field, fans call it Messi magic.

LIONEL MESSI	
Career matches played	887
Career goals	721
Career assists	344
International games played	176
International goals	104
International assists	53

LIONEL MESSI

Ronaldo played for a long time for the Spanish team Real Madrid. He's also on Portugal's national team. Both Ronaldo and Messi can score from anywhere on the field. But who is better? You decide.

CRISTIANO RONALDO	
Career matches played	978
Career goals	726
Career assists	231
International games played	201
International goals	123
International assists	33

CRISTIANO RONALDO

GLOSSARY

corner kick: a free kick from a corner of the field near the goal

counterattack: an attempt to score quickly after taking the ball from the other team

defender: a player whose job is mostly defense

forward: a player whose main job it is to score goals and be responsible for offense

foul: an action by a player that referees think is unfair or against the rules

midfielder: a player who usually stays in the middle of the field and is responsible for both offense and defense

qualifying match: a match that teams play to determine who goes on to the main tournament

semifinal: the match before the finals

tackle: a defensive play that stops a player with the ball from advancing with it

Learn More

Bolte, Mari. *FIFA*. North Mankato, MN: Norwood House, 2023.

Britannica Kids: World Cup
https://kids.britannica.com/kids/article/World-Cup/390872

Doeden, Matt. *G.O.A.T. Soccer Teams*. Minneapolis: Lerner Publications, 2021.

Kiddle: FIFA Facts for Kids
https://kids.kiddle.co/FIFA

Lilley, Matt. *FIFA World Cup*. Mendota Heights, MN: Apex, 2023.

Major League Soccer
http://www.mlssoccer.com

Smith, Charles R. *Soccer Queens*. Somerville, MA: Candlewick, 2023.

US Soccer
http://www.ussoccer.com

INDEX

PHOTO ACKNOWLEDGMENTS

Image credits: Brad Smith/ISI Photos/Getty Images, p. 4; Bob Thomas/Popperfoto/Getty Images, p. 5; Catherine Ivill/Getty Images, p. 6; Mike Hewitt/Getty Images, p. 7; Pressinphoto/Getty Images, p. 8; Cameron Spencer/Getty Images, p. 9; David Berding/Stringer/Getty Images, p. 10; Neal Simpson - EMPICS/Getty Images, p. 11; Icon Sportswire/Getty Images, pp. 12, 14, 21; Simon M Bruty/Getty Images, p. 13; Xinhua News Agency/Getty Images, p. 15; David Madison/Getty Images, p. 16; Marvin Ibo Guengoer - GES Sportfoto/Getty Images, p. 17; Stuart Franklin - FIFA /Getty Images, p. 18; Denis Doyle/Getty Images, p. 20; James Gilbert/Stringer/Getty Images, p. 22; Carmen Mandato/Getty Images, p. 23; Eurasia Sport Images/Getty Images, p. 25; Dean Mouhtaropoulos/Getty Images, p. 26; Xavier Lorenzo/Getty Images, p. 27; VI-Images/Getty Images, p. 28; Abdulaziz Alnoman/Getty Images, p. 29.

Design elements: Ali Kahfi/Getty Images; sarayut Thaneerat/Getty Images.

Cover: AP Photo/Robin Alam/Icon Sportswire.